Graeme Dixon (1955–2010) was born in Perth, Western Australia. Between the ages of ten and fourteen he lived in a Salvation Army Boys Home, before being expelled from high school. He was in and out of reformatories and at sixteen ended up in Fremantle Prison where he spent most of the next nine years. His first poetry collection, *Holocaust Island*, was written in prison and was the inaugural winner of the David Unaipon Award in 1989.

First Nations Classics

HOLOCAUST ISLAND

GRAEME DIXON

UQP

First published 1990 by University of Queensland Press
PO Box 6042, St Lucia, Queensland 4067 Australia
This First Nations Classics edition published 2023

University of Queensland Press (UQP) acknowledges the Traditional Owners
and their custodianship of the lands on which UQP operates. We pay our
respects to their Ancestors and their descendants, who continue cultural and
spiritual connections to Country. We recognise their valuable contributions
to Australian and global society.

uqp.com.au
reception@uqp.com.au

Cover design by Jenna Lee
Typeset in 11.5/14 pt Bembo Std by Post Pre-press Group, Brisbane
Printed in Australia by McPherson's Printing Group

First Nations Classics are assisted
by the Australian Government through
the Australia Council, its arts funding
and advisory body.

This project is supported by the Copyright Agency's Cultural Fund.

C©PYRIGHTAGENCY
CULTURAL FUND

A catalogue record for this book is available from the National Library of Australia.

ISBN 978 0 7022 6603 4 (pbk)
ISBN 978 0 7022 6797 0 (epdf)

To all our Brothers and Sisters
who died in custody
May their souls R.I.P.

Contents

Introduction by Ali Cobby Eckermann   ix

PRISON SPIRIT

Prison   3

Black death   6

Regrets   7

Escape!   11

Yigga's run   12

Battle heroes   21

Darryl   23

Genocide   25

Prison spirit   26

HOLOCAUST ISLAND

Doomed prophecy   29

Re-enactment   30

W.A.S.P. / S.W.A.T.   31

Six feet of land rights   33

Holocaust island   34

When   35

Home   36

Pension day   38

Single Mum   40

Where? 43

Oldies 45

$2 a bottle dreams 47

Hypocritic sponsorship 51

A unfortunate life 55

To let 59

Black magic 62

Country girl 66

Noongah girl 70

The artist 72

Broome bound 76

Glossary 79

INTRODUCTION
by Ali Cobby Eckermann

This epic collection by Graeme Dixon is an important reflection of contemporary Aboriginal life more than three decades ago. It is a poignant, poetic portrayal of hardship in a disadvantaged life while facing the constant threat of violence by the Australian police force. Many of the poems are written in basic form – streetwise and honest. Perhaps the tone is further influenced by prison talk, as Graeme spent much of his early life in the cycle of incarceration.

While inside, he witnessed the endemic killing of Aboriginal prisoners by the police and prison officers, including a reference to Robert (Walker), the Kokatha poet, who was murdered in Fremantle Prison in 1984. This collection is dedicated to all those Brothers and Sisters (RIP) and there are many. Deaths in custody and Land Rights are two of the major issues that remain unrepented for and unresolved by each and every Australian government who have held power, and diminished their promises for reform.

Jack Davis AM (RIP), the esteemed Noongar poet and playwright, wrote the original foreword to *Holocaust Island* in 1990. Graeme Dixon was also Noongar, born in Perth in 1955. His parents separated when he was very young, resulting in Graeme and his siblings spending time in Sister Kate's Home and the Salvation Army orphanage. Most of his younger life was spent in institutions.

He once stated that he started writing to: 'get things off [his] chest' and, unfortunately, he destroyed most of these early writings because: '[He] didn't feel safe with [his] feelings lying around … for prying eyes.'

At twenty-five Graeme decided to keep out of jail. He battled with alcohol and drugs until he met his wife, Sharmaine, who recognised his talent as a writer and urged him to further his education. So, at age twenty-seven, Graeme enrolled as a tertiary student at the University of Western Australia. Later he completed a course at Curtin University and sometimes lectured on Aboriginal history and social justice issues. Sadly, Graeme died in Perth in 2010.

His family remembers Graeme lovingly as a man with a beautiful and rich heart who gave more than he had. Every time they were together their big brother would always share memories of their childhood years and his siblings witnessed how his writing took him away from the hardships he had endured. He loved Sharmaine and their son, Jordy, very much, and in his own right was very loved by his brothers and sisters, nieces and nephews, and family, and by all who knew him. Central to this universe is their sweet mother.

Always deep in reflection, Graeme was dedicated to his writing and his devotion to the truth-seeking justice for the rights of his people. His family dedicate these words to him: 'Though we will forever miss the beauty of his earthly presence nonetheless our brother's spiritual essence lives deep within our hearts forever.' The republication of *Holocaust Island* is a true blessing to them all.

Often we remind ourselves of how much progress Aboriginal Australia has achieved since 1989 – and we would be correct. However, the subjects that have been documented in these raw and honest writings highlight the many issues that have not progressed to an equitable level. In many regions of Australia these social problems continue, such as overcrowding, low income, lack of employment opportunity, and constant addiction to dull this socioeconomic pain. For those living an existence that is harrowingly described here, Graeme's writings are an emotional mirror to what many Aboriginal people still experience today. Graeme's poetry is vivid and essential against the mainstream media that wants to highlight First Nations' success and use tragedy and trauma as a manoeuvre for political sway.

Between the lines is a plea for freedom, a cessation from the society that has pushed Aboriginal people to a new brink of existence. In the distance remains the knowledge of life before white occupation on this land. There are verses that describe the desperation of caring for others in such difficult times of social exclusion, while mourning the existence of cultural freedom and respect. The sagas described here carry a hymnal of sorrow and regret, and the constant appeal for a caring justice while still alive. It is a heavy statement that contains: *then when the reaper comes / to switch off our lights / our souls may rest in peace, knowing / at last! Six feet of land rights.*

These words have no frills. Read the poems slowly. Grasp at the realism of this historical review. Grasp this gift of history with the sincerity in which it was written. As you turn each page, hold the tenacity of witness. Graeme Dixon has penned his bravery to survive on these pages. Celebrate that survival continues, as it has and always will, enduring the confusion and cruelty that exists on Holocaust Island.

Holocaust Island won the inaugural David Unaipon Award in 1989 and sits proudly alongside the writings of the judges, Oodgeroo Noonuccal, Jack Davis and Mudrooroo.

PRISON SPIRIT

Prison

Prison
what a bitch
Brutality
Savageness
Depression
Is all caused by it
Must'a been
A wajella
Who invented this Hell
Wouldn't know
For sure
But by the torture
I can tell

To deny
A man freedom
Is the utmost
Form of
Torment
Just for
The crime
Of finding money
To pay
The Land lord's rent
Justice for all
That is
Unless you're poor

Endless days
Eternal nights
Thinking
Worrying
In a concrete box
The disease
It causes
In the head –
I'd rather
Have the pox

Because man
Is just
An animal
Who needs to see
The stars
Free as birds
In the sky
Not through
These iron bars

There must be
Another way
To punish
Penalise
Those of us
Who stray
And break
The rules

That protect
The taxpayers
From us
The reef
Of humanity's
Wrecks.

Black death

For forty thousand years, our ancestors
Caressed our fertile seed
and tended to the weaning
Gave us life then we were freed
a living part of Dreaming
encased in living flesh
But now the fruit is hanging
in cells of bars and mesh.

Now those links eternal chains
have been torn asunder
as the guns in Whitey's hands
spat lightning flash and thunder.

They sat midst the dirt and flies
alone and in disgrace
But behind those saddened eyes
are angry words and screaming
aimed at those in uniforms
who killed those of the Dreaming.

Regrets

I started stealing cars
at fourteen-years old
Trying to impress me mates
Proving I was bold
Flying around in V.8.s
Baiting the manatj
Jesus! life was exciting
Full of thrills, spills 'n' laughs
When I did get caught
Didn't worry me at all!
I knew I'd only spend
A coupla weeks in Longmore
And it wouldn't take too long
To be back on the streets
Prowling for cars to steal
Manatj to defeat
My teenage years flew past
In and out of trouble
Never realising
White law would burst my bubble
but it finally happened
When officially I became a man
The magistrate gave me
Eighteen months in Freo can

Shit! That sentence stung
Dulling the fire in my eyes
One of me mates escaped
Via prison cell necktie
I tried to convince him
A coupla months ain't long
But it was no bloody use
His spirit had already gone
It's hard for any man
To be caged in a prison cell
But if your skin is black
It's like burning in hell
Being locked up by wajellas
Glaring at you with hate
Counting down the hours
To your earliest release date

But as the bible says
'All things come to pass'
My time eventually came
To be free at last
My experiences caused me
To attempt a brand new life
With no more thieving
Or getting into strife
I confidently set out
Searching for a job
I had even decided
To avoid me old mob

but everywhere I asked
I got for an answer
'May we have a look
At your driver's licence sir?'

My past had returned
Haunting me like a spook
I couldn't find no work
No matter how hard I looked
This made me finally decide
To visit the dreaded police
Asking politely if I could
Sit for a driver's licence please
The copper's sarcastic reply
Was poison to me ears
'Look here fella
You're suspended for five years!'
My suspensions as a juvenile
I had truly forgot
And waiting for five years
It seemed I'd probably rot!
So to secure reliable work
I began to drive cars
That my friends is the reason
I'm back behind prison bars
Counting the endless days
For the next coupla years
Missing freedom, friends and family
Shedding lonesome tears

If you young black fellows
Have any kind of sense
Be patient and behave
Get your driver's licence
Waiting to turn seventeen
Isn't really very long
And it's a long lonely journey
Down the road that is wrong.

Escape!

Spiteful rifle spits
slices through still night
Fragile life flickers
dying beneath searchlight
Faceless, uniformed figure
caresses hot, faithful toy
Warm blood gushes
shattered skull, tender boy.

Institutionalised keepers
blood lusted by the kill
gaze upon the carcass
Overwhelming power thrills!
Nobody mentions
victims a hungry thief
fallen from life's tree
like browned autumn leaf.

World eternally spinning
nothing breaks this move
Deafening silence returning
prison's eerie gloom
Bloody razor-wire glistens
beneath silvery moon
Night, quietly mourning
life escaped too soon.

Yigga's run

Bugger this for a joke coord!
I'm hitting the toe
Jail's breaking my heart
and making me low
My yorga's pissed off
with this bunji wajella bloke
on all this bottled anger
I'm ready to choke
I haven't had a visit
near on six months now
so I'm gunna chase the moon
and I know exactly how
I've got this appeal
due to be heard
it'll be knocked back
coz the judge is a turd
But if manatj give me
a smidgen of a break
it'll be a risky chance
I'm prepared to take
I'll start training tomorrow
or better still tonight
to be fit as a fiddle
and ready to fight

'Yigga to the grill!
Get ready for the court!'
Well this is finally it
my brain nervously thought
Shit, shower and shave
then into caged prison van
butterflies fluttering in guts
hoping that I can
take full advantage
of opportunities coming my way
remembering the cliché
'All are famous for one day'

Escorted to the cells
in the Supreme Court bowels
dark, dingy and dank
full of smells so foul
Slyly I slipped off tie
sticking it in me pocket
I had this flimsy plan
piss weak but don't knock it

They called out my name
To get myself prepared
I was bracing my institutionalised brain
beyond the realms of care
They cuffed both my wrists
and led me on out
I gave manatj a glance

both were stocky and stout
Up steep wooden stairs
the manatj escorted me
all thoughts in my head
were only of being free
We sat on a hard wooden bench
outside the courtroom
I was trying to shake off
premonitions of doom
'Do ya's mind if I smoke?'
I asked one of the police
My frayed, tangled nerves
I hoped nicotine would ease
The manatj answered 'No,
but ya better make it quick
I'm certain your name
will be called in a tick'
I said I didn't care
if my appeal succeeded or not
as in six months time
I'd be free on the trot
'I've done three years'
I added with reckless grin
'and another six months
is not original sin
and jail don't hurt much
if you stay relaxed
at least in prison a man
don't get his pay taxed!'

Both manatj just smiled
Seemingly more at ease
neither appeared to jerry
that I was on the sleaze
'Do ya's reckon it's possible
to take off the cuffs
so I can put on me tie
and look less of a scruff?'
They stared each other
in the eyeballs
one shrugged his shoulders
saying 'no worries at all'
I put on wrinkled tie
forced smile on face
deep down in my chest
my heart fairly raced

'John Yigga to room one'
the court bailiff called
on hearing these words
poor heart nearly stalled
'Well, here ya go Yigga'
The manatj said to me
'you'll soon find out
what the appeal judge decrees'
We walked into court
silent as a grave
I was breathing deep and hard
trying to be brave

The court clerk hit his hammer
Shouting 'all ye stand!'
Wigged, owl-like judge entered
self-righteous and grand
'So you're appealing Mr Yigga'
he said down to me
with sarcastic look in his eye
'against sentence severity
Well, I'm real sorry son
I see no solid grounds
and for this fundamental reason
your appeal is stood down'

As they led me away
I thought 'here I go'
at last this is it
I'm hitting the toe
One cop had hold of me
by the left arm
his grip was relaxed
and he seemed to be calm
The other copper walked
a few feet ahead
suddenly I broke the grasp
and for freedom I fled

They pursued my elusive body
straight out the front door
shouting 'Stop you crazy bastard

in the name of the law!'
Into the court carpark
bending low I flew
trying to think clearly
of what I must do
A half dozen angry manatj
fell in on my trail
but my stamina was ready
through exercise in jail
'Stop that dangerous man!'
the manatj yelled out
to the curious citizens
frozen by their shout
But I was through the park
and entering the street
Two exhausted coppers gave in
I had now four to beat
'Go like the wind bro!'
a Noongah kid yelled to me
'Spring like the Bungarra
if you want to be free!'
I crossed the road
like a roo in full flight
my heart was fairly skipping
me lungs were feeling tight
But suddenly a hairy hand
grabbed desperately at my shoulder
my body felt so weak
'twas heavy as a boulder

I reached into my soul
and begged for a little more
from the stamina I had stored
but I had nearly used it all
'I've got you now mate!'
I heard the manatj angrily say
'I run marathons for a hobby
I could do this all day'

So I stopped in my tracks
abruptly bending low
Catapulting over my body
I watched the copper go
He did a half somersault
landing with a heavy thump
I quickly straightened up
and over him I jumped
Instantly his hand shot up
grabbing me by the ankle
quickly pulling out his cuffs
within seconds I was manacled
I lay prone with sweat pissing
blowing like a beached whale
gloomy realisation setting in
I was heading back to jail
The copper breathed heavily
'That was a stupid try
now you're coming with me
back to the pigsty'

Once I was in the lock-up
I then began to shit
deep in my heart I knew
I was going to be hit
'Make fools of us will ya!'
a copper angrily said
'If I had me gun then
right now you'd be dead!'
The first blow landed
with a knee to the thigh
followed in quick succession
by punches to the eyes
'Strip the mongrel down!'
The duty sergeant yelled
'Then chuck him bare-arsed naked
into the cooling cell!'
They roughly threw me in
as naked as a jay
for my little excursion
I knew I'd dearly pay
A bucketful of water
was thrown over me
for a man is most vulnerable
when cold and naggedy
They turned on the fan
embedded in the roof
my nose was fairly bleeding
I spat out a broken tooth
I shivered and shook

through the cold and the fear
but I wouldn't give them
the satisfaction of a tear
The cell door flew open
in strode four burly cops
who systematically beat my body
I thought they'd never stop
When their revenge was sated
I was bruised and bloody raw
On departure one turned and spat
'Don't mess with the law!'

They found weary body hanging
later that lonely night
spirit finally broken
no longer desiring a fight
All this Noongah life lived
sneering at the gun
but this time it fired
jolted by Yigga's run
Was it the Queen's manatj
or could it have been he?
Nobody really gives a shit
but at least his soul is free.

Battle heroes

You bucked an evil system
putting up hell of a fight
struggling brave and hard
against the captors' agressive spite
So they savagely beat your bodies
whilst chained to the ground
For what logical reason?
Because your skin was brown!
Though the body's strength was sapped
ancient spirits fought on
so fragile throats were compressed
till all signs of life had gone
Other mortal injuries from battle
severe enough to cause death
cracked head!
bullet hole!
strangulation!
all took away life's sweet breath

State paid doctors and police
ruled against you of course!
coming to neutral judgements
'reasonable bloody force!'
And this informed Noongah people
the state sanctions this war
so fight in self defence
you're not protected by Queen's law

Though they lost this battle
warriors brave and bold
the survivors will not rest
till injustice has been resolved
for 'all is fair in love and war'
is the invaders' battle-cry
So defy this oppression
or we're all destined to die

And Yagan is still the hero
pioneer of our righteous cause
(will always be remembered
with respectful, silent pause)
But there's a new breed of martyr
who in bloody battle fell
Maori Tony, Robert and Charlie
John Pat and young Ricky as well.

Darryl

Though the town's forgotten
I remember well
a skinny half-caste kid
hanging in a cell
Your body was caught
in the pain of life
and the agonised throes
of violent strife
We were all stunned
with terror and fear
those of us left who loved you so dear
There will never ever
be time to forget
your agonised face
and that leather boot lace
They cut your shell down
gave it respect
more than they gave you in life
when proudly erect
But you were a child
a product of time
a little bit lost a little bit wild
loving and gentle, slightly uncouth
They refused you the right
to outgrow your youth

But I remember you Darryl
your humour your smile
the good times we shared
for a space and a while
and sometimes when I'm down
and alone in the night
I wonder what would have been
had they treated you right
If you were alive
you would be thirty today
maybe contentedly watching
your children at play.

Genocide

Two hundred years
of white occupation
Two hundred years
of BLACK desolation
Two hundred years
on the Europeans' menu
A million bloody tears
still the genocide continues.

They got rid of us
down in Tasmania
Now they're trying in
the rest of Australia
Why we plead
we are a race of so few
Are we beasts to cull
or are we human too

They cry for the BLACKS
deep in SOUTH AFRICA
They cry for the oppressed
in the jungles of NICARAGUA
Why don't they cry
for us in this HELL
instead of chaining lynching
in cold prison cells?

Prison spirit

Gazed into holes
a brim full of souls
that had dried black
stretched on a rack.

Wallowing in pain
one suddenly grinned
and everything thinned
as he became sane.

Kick me he said
I am not dead
I can still cope
there will always be hope
while my mind
has its freedom.

I am no beast
I know at least
I have a free mind
that's the best kind
that's me –
I am free.

HOLOCAUST ISLAND

Doomed prophecy

Tall warrior standing erect
Proud chin held high
A manner to defy
Scarred chest fully expanded
Back, straight and strong
Gazing out to sea
At a shape that was alien
To an ancient memory
Says down to his yorga
Standing sheltered in his shadow
'I feel a change, Kirra,
Is about to come'
But he smiled
For he knew
They had eternity on their side

Re-enactment

They sailed around the world
In sailing ships of old
They sailed around the world
Cruel, unrelenting, bold
They came a second time
These men with golden locks
They came a second time
Bringing alcohol and pox
But this time they didn't kill
with muskets or with swords
This time they didn't kill
In the name of Holy Lords
Because the world was watching
This re-enactment fleet
Because the world was watching
They trod with careful feet
They prefer to keep it secret
When they murder and they burn
But now the party's over
The killing will return
But now the party's over
for the dead our mothers yearn

W.A.S.P. / S.W.A.T.
White Anglo/Saxon Protestants
Special Weapons And Tactics

Barnstorming striking troopers
with naked violent hearts
kicking down our front doors
tearing us apart
Threatening all our people
with fully loaded guns
blowing out the fragile brains
of our defenceless sons

And still they expect us
to have and show respect
while they act like klansmen
a new elitist sect
treating us as vermin
who need eradication
That seems to be the reason
they want confrontation
We too demand the basic rights
of people in this land
But they never seem to give
but order and demand
that we play the justice game
then they make the rules
and if we speak up and protest
we're looked upon as fools

All we want is justice
we know the proper way
to stand tall, defend ourselves
in court and have our say
But what white justice seems to do
is to send out racist gangs
Meanwhile in jails around the land
our young they die and hang.

And white Australia you at large
say we have a complex
Don't you read the papers
or couldn't you care less
This country's first born People
are in a trap of genocide
Agh! you, you wouldn't give a shit if all
Black Australians died.

Six feet of land rights

If we never succeed in reclaiming our country
doomed to live life paying rent to the gentry
It would be a good thing if after our death day
for that six feet of earth we didn't have to pay
It would ease the pressure, on those of our kind
Poor, mourning, sad people, left living behind
It would make the last day easier to face
if that financial burden was lifted
from our poverty-ridden race
Then when the reaper comes
to switch off our lights
our souls may rest in peace, knowing
at last! Six feet of land rights.

Holocaust island

Nestled in the Indian Ocean
Like a jewel in her crown
The worshippers of Babel come
To relax and turn to brown
To recuperate from woe and toil
and leave their problems far behind
To practice ancient rituals
The habits of their kind

But what they refuse to realise
Is that in this little Isle
are skeletons in their cupboards
of deeds most foul and vile
Far beneath this Island's surface
In many an unmarked place
lie the remnants of forgotten ones
Kia, members of my race.

When
(in retrospect)

When the colour of a person's skin
Is as unimportant
As the colour of his eyes
When politicians stop
Deceiving our people
With the telling
Of their white lies
When the breed
Sired by convicts
Cease to worship
The invader
Captain Cook
When they return
To our People
The Sacred lands
They took
When compensation
Is paid in full
For the atrocities
Of 200 years past
Then and only then
Oppressors
Will our Ancestors
Rest in peace at last.

Home

Where do you come from?
a stranger once asked me
He said he hailed from Scotland
miles across deep blue sea
Where is your homeland,
he continued curious,
and was bitter sweet departure
sentimental but glorious?
He said he missed Scotland
and pined to return
asked if for home
my heart often yearned?
I yearn for those Green Hills,
he splashed with a tear
And dying on foreign shores
was his deepest fear
What about you son,
he enquired absently,
in the warmth of your home
would you rather be?
Then he went silent
and gazed into my eye
begging me for an answer
I started with a sigh

I have no sweet home sir
where I can run free
no place to hang my hat
you see
I am Aborigine

Pension day

The natives are restless
in their State Housing homes
Unmarried mothers
are no longer alone
Relations are arriving
from near and afar
Social Security pensioner
today you're a star

Anxious glances
are cast up the street
Postie has a timetable
he never ever keeps
Dad swears one day
he'll wring his white neck
Mum says don't worry
he'll lob in a sec

Young yorga's dream
of new jeans and shoes
Young men scheme
to cadge money for booze
Petrol for cars
more than two dollars worth
Then it's off to the TAB
To invest in the turf

Even dogs and kids
are running amok
they know boya will fly
when the oldies are drunk
Cokes and lollies
and everything nice
Wishin' wouldn't it be moorditj
if pension days fell twice

Postie has been
cheques have been changed
Food and drink
have been all arranged
Dad cracks a bottle
passes it around
Says let's have a charge
then piss off to town

Town she jumps
on pension day nights
Girls looking for boys
boys looking for fights
Tomorrow they'll be hungover
some sore – most quiet
But who gives a shit
coz tonight Noongahs RIOT!

Single Mum

She awakens every other morn
to cries of empty-bellied kids
tries feeding them with little
as they reckon Jesus Christ once did
She spends most the morning
getting them fed, clean and dressed
Holding back tears of frustration
for her is an emotional test.

The State rents her a concrete box
in an outer suburban slum
they promise her a house one day
she feels this will never come
for now she's gotta try make do
meeting the rent and other bills
if the loneliness don't get her
depression eventually will.

In winter it's cold as ice
in summer as hot as hell
the plumbing always playing up
there's a cockroach plague as well
There's no carpet on hard floors
old sheets are used as curtains
but she has new locks on doors
around here women can't be certain.

The suburb that she lives in
is rife with vandalism and crime
she's virtually a prisoner in a cell
never venturing out night-time
If her kids wander out of sight
she'll frantically shout their names out
Everyone says she's a worrier
she knows there are deviants about.

She often dreams of the love
she gave in her youthful years
but tries blocking these memories
they only lead to tears
Still she'll forever remember the day
she awoke to a cold empty bed
wondering eternally if it was her
was she the reason why he fled.

Trying to forget those painful times
has developed a valium habit
any painkillers coming her way
alcohol, drugs, she'll grab it
She knows she must stop one day
but the wounds are far too raw
and it's never knowing, that hurts
what the future holds in store.

The only sunshine in her life
is on fortnightly pension days
the whole block then seems to smile
and rellies come around to stay
Sometimes even long lost lovers
arrive to visit the deserted wives
but that's the only sip of water
in the arid desert of their lives.

So the struggle to survive
stumbles from one day to the next
She wishes they prepared her for this
in High School life skills text
She often contemplates suicide
as the only escape from this pit
But a kiss and cuddle from the kids
makes her think maybe it'll be worth it.

Where?

Where have they gone
I often wonder
Those great Southern Tribes
Where is the culture
the lore
the legends
those haunting didgeridoo vibes
Where are the grey old ones
to educate
to enlighten
the youth in the ways of old
Where has it all gone
the traditions
the land
has it all been stolen and sold
Surely they have left us a little
those invading Europeans
Just a place
to call sweet home
and fulfil our Noongah dreams
Or is it far too late
to worry
to wish
our lifestyle had remained unchanged

And do we have to learn
to live
to survive
in a world that's been rearranged?

Oldies

The far away looks
in their wrinkled faded eyes
No longer interested
in the world outside
They'd rather gaze inward
to the memory's reminiscence
of a long forgotten tribe
Though reality is dirty streets
they still see their land
picturing rolling hills
and red desert sand
Hunters and gatherers
stalking grey kangaroo
Making wild oat dampers
and wallaby stew
Sitting around fires
under the dreaming stars
Bush sounds in the night
uninterrupted by cars
Listening to the stories
of forty-thousand years
When they recollect them now
they fight back the tears
Waking in the morning
to an unpolluted dawn
Alive and beautiful
like a new baby born

With warriors departing
on an early day stalk
No rushing or bustling
just a leisurely bush walk
The women and children
gather through the day
while women toil
children happily play
Wise old grey ones
chatter and sing
Through well-earned respect
they're treated like kings

But now they sadly realise
those innocent years have passed
Shattered and destroyed
when that first fleet anchor cast
Now the old ones
have no land to return to
They just waste slowly away
in a state owned ghetto
And on death they will take
the last links with the Dreaming
While an uninterested youth
learn the white man's scheming.

$2 a bottle dreams

When the world
that surrounds me
seems at its brutal worst
When my brain
throbbingly expands
ready to burst
When the Government man
threatens
to haul me away
When before my eyes
I see my hair
turning grey
That's when I must go
to my local
Dream-maker
in the main street
near the butcher
and baker
To ask,
sick to death
of so-called normality,
for a potion
to distance me
from reality
He smiles at me
with greedy
glint of eye

Listens to my problems
with false
understanding sighs
Advises me
to slow down
ease off life's throttle
then sells me
my dreams
two dollars a bottle
In my
induced dreams
it is an undivided nation
No bigotry,
prejudice
or racial discrimination
No looking down
noses
at gentle original tribes
Towards our
Asian neighbours
no antagonistic vibes
With politicians
truly united
for the benefit of all
Society
no longer classified
into the rich
and the poor
Greedy

multinationals
no longer environmentally
maim
Reconditioning
land and forests
to before the
Europeans came
And all of our children
laugh sing dance and play
assured
that tomorrow
will bear forth
a new day

But then I awake
feeling remorse and hungover
when the realisation sets in
that my dreamtime is over
Being blatantly
stared at
by the taxpayers who pass
When I catch their eyes
they look away
downcast
Because it's my kind
lying sprawled in the park
that's a reminder
of Australia's history
so dark

With all
to look forward to
but my next pension day
I slowly arise
and stagger away
and no matter
how escapist
to all it may seem
it's what
keeps me going
my $2 a bottle dreams

Hypocritic sponsorship

This TRULY MAGNIFICENT
SPORTING SPECTACULAR
is so PROUDLY
BROUGHT TO YOU BY
cirrhosis of the liver
BREWERIES,
THE LAGER
THAT REAL MEN BUY!
In conjunction with
the COMPANY
THAT GAVE YOU
lung cancer cigarettes
And JUST FOR YOU
gambling folk,
THE STATE HAS SUPPLIED
FACILITIES TO BET
We'd also PROUDLY
like to remind you that
the MANAGEMENT of these
AUSTRALIAN COMPANIES
have DONATED
A BIG FAT CHEQUE!
to HELP stamp-out
MARIJUANA DEALERS
and JUNKIE WRECKS

Because, with
DEEP SYMPATHY,
they realise
that DRUGS RUIN LIVES
of INNOCENT KIDS!
And this country
WON'T BE SAFE
till ALL FORMS
OF ADDICTION
have been rid!
Also,
they are opening
a TRUST FUND
in the not too
distant future time
TO AID A CAUSE
THAT NEEDS
PUBLIC SUPPORT!
A FREE
suicidal assistance
telephone line
And you women
in the audience
don't worry,
you've not been
left out,
as they're starting
a CRISIS CENTRE

FOR THOSE LADIES
WHOSE DRUNK HUBBIES
knock them about
And also
YOU BEAUTIFUL KIDS
they have
A PROJECT
JUST FOR YOU'S
They will GIVE
two cents an empty,
so make sure
your folks
DRINK MORE BOOZE!
Lung cancer cigarettes
have a SCHOLARSHIP
AVAILABLE
FOR THE FUTURE
All you
have to do
IS SMOKE
their teenage label
And finally
the MINISTER reminds you
that these
companies
HELP fill
state coffers
and the money

IS NEEDED
BY THE PEOPLE
NO MATTER WHAT
is said
by the COMMUNIST scoffers.

A unfortunate life

Born in the country
well, not exactly in
more on the fringe
in a hession humpy
near a dry river
by decree of dominant law
no longer a nomadic liver
Innocent childhood years
flew too swiftly past
innocence replaced
by tears and fears
when realisation set in
that he differed
as did the rest of his kin
from the wajella kids
who played in town
at night he shamefully regretted
his skin was so brown
Attempted education
deserted it too soon
Understood English
except strange words
like coon
boong turd
black nigger

Seemed life was
black gun to temple
white finger squeezing trigger.

On becoming a man
mum said 'go!'
'leave this cruel land
for you to live
to survive
you must desert our clan
as this white man's town
full of prejudice and shame
will keep you down
as long as they can see
your skin is so brown'
He died a little
he cried a lot
the day they sent him away
He begged his father
'Let me stay
I'd much rather live
the Noongahs' way'
But dad remained strict
'Your future is lost
in your home town
you'll always be bossed
and pushed around
Go to the city
live with Aunty Vi

there's no guarantees
but give it a try'
Reluctantly he left
his family so sad
That land may not be his
but it was all he had
a feeling
an instinct
deep in his heart –
to that land
he was a vital part

City life
what a mistake!
Racism rife
worse than the bush
Tried to find work
without any success
so with other lost lads
around pubs he lurked
Aunty couldn't afford
six kids and him
'I'll move out'
he told her on whim
'Karne! My nephew'
She said angrily
'You're my sister's son
your blood flows through me'
But still he went

with a fragment of pride
a legacy of ancestors
now on the other side
to live in the parks
by city riverbanks
where after dark
he joined the homeless ranks

Harassed by police
like all parkies are
there was no peace
sleeping under neon stars
Life became a cycle
of crime, wine and jail time
He finally realised
there was no happy ends
he decided to abandon
his derelict friends

They found him one day
suspended from a tree
In a grave he now lays
Nodytch!
but eternally free.

To let

Nice flat to let
the rental notice said
that's partly furnished
with large double bed
scenic ocean views
in a small quiet block
close to the port
near the south dock

I give it a ring
in the early morn
we needed a place
before baby was born
'come over and view'
the caretaker said
so I got the Mrs
out of mum's bed

'A home of our own'
she blissfully sighed
'I dearly wish
no one else has applied'
'Don't worry sweetheart'
I said confident
'I've got a good job
to settle the rent'

As soon as he saw us
it showed in his eyes
the critical look
the sarcastic sigh
'I'm sorry mate'
he said with a smirk
'we only rent
to those who work'

'I am employed!'
I answered frustrated
'and the finance companies
have me highly rated'
'That's not the point'
he said without tact
'the real problem is
we don't let to Blacks!'

So I hit him hard
on his fat chin
I was sick to death
of blatant racism
'Why don't they say'
I asked my wife why
'in the rental pages
Blacks need not apply'

But now I've found
a room of my own
The worry is
my wife is alone
in a women's refuge
I hope she is well
and as safe as me
in my prison cell

Black magic

They spotted him one day
kicking a ball around
The way he bobbed 'n' weaved
and flew above the ground
gave them just a hint
of his natural talent and skills
All they had to do
was lure him from those hills.

He was a quiet, shy man
as dark as fertile earth
born in the bush
he's never been to Perth
Built like a gum tree
he played fair but hard
that's when he wasn't tempted
by wine, women, and cards.

So they offered him a bribe
like Captain Cook once did
to move to the city
and become their new star kid
'Can my family come with me?'
he enquired, still naive
'No, but they can visit
when we give you monthly leave.'

But later in the city he thought
training's sure a prick
especially when a man's lonely
friendless and homesick
Jesus! He'd often think
I'd trade in my left eye
just for a little nibble
of mum's kangaroo meat pie.

Pre-season training slowly passed
and winter soon began
He played a lousy first game
was booed off by the fans
'Where'd ya leave ya black heart,
in flaming San Francisco!'
He seemed to spend the match
running blindly to and fro.
'Don't worry none kid'
his sympathetic coach later said
'When ya finally get your feet
you'll kill 'em all stone dead.'

The next game's opponents
were old traditional foes
a tough and skillful mob
who always loved to pose
The bloke he was playing on
glared at him and sniggered
'Jesus, holy flaming Christ

I've got me a bloody nigger!'
Those acid words made something
deep inside him click

So systematically
he dazzled that bloke
with Black fellow magic
He dodged, he ducked, he weaved
he took screaming marks
and he booted that leather ball
right out of the footy park
His rival angrily whispered
'I'm going to get you Sport!'
A shirt front to this man
was his silent, but deadly, retort
The enemy came rushing in
to assist a fallen mate
but Noongah'd sped off towards goal
they'd arrived seconds too late
The big, ornery, half-back sneered
'Come on, try and pass!'
So with bone crushing hip and shoulder
he sat him on ample arse
He then bullet-passed the ball
over to his resting rover
who booted the winning goal
just as the game was over.

They chaired him from the ground
as the final siren blared
he was a bloody heavy bastard
but no one really cared
Black Magic! Black Magic!
as one the big crowd roared
but no smile
there was
on Noongah's face
as above the mob he soared
Was it worth his effort
to be wajella's hero for a day?
Right then he decided to return home
he no longer desired to play.

Country girl

for Sharmaine

I've been living
in the city
near on fifteen years
or more
And still the neon
shines brighter
than any star
I ever saw
But every
now and then when
the wind blows
from the east
I think back
to my childhood
these memories
have never ceased

To endless fields
of golden wheat
that disappear
into clear blue sky
The squawking of
white cockatoos
as a flock
flies screeching by
Long winding

red gravelled road
leading to
lonely homestead
Feeling the ever present
spirit of Noongahs
both those living
and those dead
A mob of skinny
cousins and mates
playing chasey
through the trees
Jumping and dodging
laughing and screaming
dogs nipping
at boney knees
Dark brown wrinkled
grey-haired oldies
spinning ancient yarns
under shady gums
Though we'd heard them
many times
when they beckoned
we'd quickly come
My dark and handsome
tall strong dad
had such gnarled
blistered hands
possessed a thirst
for demon drink

earned via working
a hard dry land
My pretty and proud
hard toiling mum
whose face always
wore a frown
But us kids
were never worried
just as long as
she was around
Although we always
seemed so poor
we were rich
in other ways
We never worried
about tomorrow
being interested
only in today
Time seemed unimportant then
we never ever
rushed around
We always took it
slow and easy
in our sleepy
wheatbelt town

Those days seem
so far away
yet they're vivid
in my mind
always stored
in my heart
as secret mementos
of my kind
Though I'm now
a city girl
who likes to party
dance and sing
Deep down inside
my country heart
I'm just a kid
from Quairading

Noongah girl

Cool southerly
on midsummer's days
Fresh sea mist
on south western bays
Smooth blue lakes
on windless afternoons
Exhilarating cold rain
in the middle of June
Beauty of nature
puts my head
my heart
in uncontrolled whirl
reminds me of you
Earth's eldest daughter
Raw sugar
Wild honey
Sweet Noongah girl

A voice like
forest parrots
that beautifully sing
Colourful as
native flowers
that bloom in spring
Seductive motion
of the waterfall
that passionately flows

Soft velvet petals
of a wild desert rose
Beauty of nature
puts my head
my heart
in uncontrolled whirl
reminds me of you
Earth's eldest daughter
Raw sugar
Wild honey
Sweet Noongah girl

The artist

I was sitting in the pub one day
sinking coldies with some mates
when the topic of conversation swung
to black artists and how they rate
It seemed to be agreed unanimously
that Namatjira was easily the best
'til I mentioned an artist I knew
who'd give poor ol' Albert a test
A cynical mate say 'spit it out
tell us of this extremely gifted bloke'
So I took a long pull on me drink
then slowly rolled meself a smoke

'Of all the Aboriginal artists I know
there's one that stands right out
the skinny fellow at the end of the bar
Yeah – the one that never shouts
He does his paintings with the tongue
colouring in with imagination
His artistry always reaches its peak
when in the state of intoxication
One of his most famous works
has been exhibited throughout the state
The piece of him outrunning a bushfire
smashing the four minute mile rate
Because of the running in the heat
sweat was fairly pissing out

so much in fact – believe it or not
it drenched the flaming fire out!

Another work that stimulates my mind
is in the dying seconds of a footy game
His team was down by just one goal
and losing would've been to shame!
The artist grabbed the ball from the centre
kicking it as hard as bloody hell
so hard in fact the darn thing burst
scoring a point and a goal as well!'

I rested then for just a spell
to have a sip and long deep drag
One of me mates blurted 'love me drunk
you're lying you dirty rotten dag!'

I give him my famous dugite leer
with nary a smile on stony face
spat to death I was talking fact
then continued at a leisurely pace

Of the time the artist was cruising along
a nor'west highway late at night
when he hit a big red kangaroo
giving them both a hell of a fright!
He said the roo sailed through the air
smashing through front windscreen
coming to rest in the back of the car

'twas the strangest thing he'd ever seen
But nothing could be as weird
as his next imaginative colouration
but he swears it's true on his mum's grave
(she must be cursed to eternal damnation)
He said the roo just shook its head
sat up and swore a bloody oath
grabbed a stubby from his box
then poured it down his throat –

'I've been hopping around this poxy land
for near on twenty years or more
outrunning roo dogs and shooting mobs
beating all they had in store
but knock me down if I'm lying
this is the closest I've ever been
to winding up as dingo bait
a destiny in which I ain't too keen!'

The artist claimed he was speechless
as the roo continued rambling on
But what really pissed him off
was that the roo had finished his carton!
'Ya reckon you could drop me off'
the roo asked now half pissed
'Fifty K's further up the road
where lives this doe that's never been kissed'

Usually on finishing this masterpiece
he'd plead his throat was mighty dry
cadge the price of a beer
and scull it down with a contented sign

So the next time you hear them argue
which Aboriginal artist is the smartest
remind them of this cruel skinny man
the world champion bullshit artist!

Broome bound

Give me an old
Holden to mend
An open road
that has no end
A couple of bucks
to buy some juice
Face me North
then let me loose
All I need
for travelling mates
is me dog, guitar
and hand of fate
Together we'll go
side by side
Heading for Broome's
Shinju tide.

We won't starve
along the way
Rellies will give us
a place to stay
Or we'll catch
a kangaroo
and use mum's recipe
for stew
Camping under
stars at night

me and dog
will be alright
Singing reggae
under the moon
me and guitar both out of tune.

When we finally
get to Broome
we won't worry about a room
as all we'll need
we can reach on the dune
of Cable Beach
We'll sing and dance
and party at night
because in Broome
the vibes are right
Sculling beer
at the old Roebuck
I hope the dog
don't get too drunk

Then one morn
I'll wake hungover
And realise,
the game is over
Then I'll beg
for a counter cheque
and head back South
what the heck!

But next year
in winter's gloom,
my heart will warm again
for Broome.

Glossary

boya – money
Bungarra – racehorse goanna
bunji – man who pays women for sexual pleasure
coord (coorda) – mate, friend
Kia – Yes
karne (karn ya) – foolish, weak
manatj – police
moorditj – good
nodytch – dead, the departed
Noongah – south-western Aboriginal person
wajella – white person
Yagan – Aboriginal freedom fighter
yorga – girl, woman